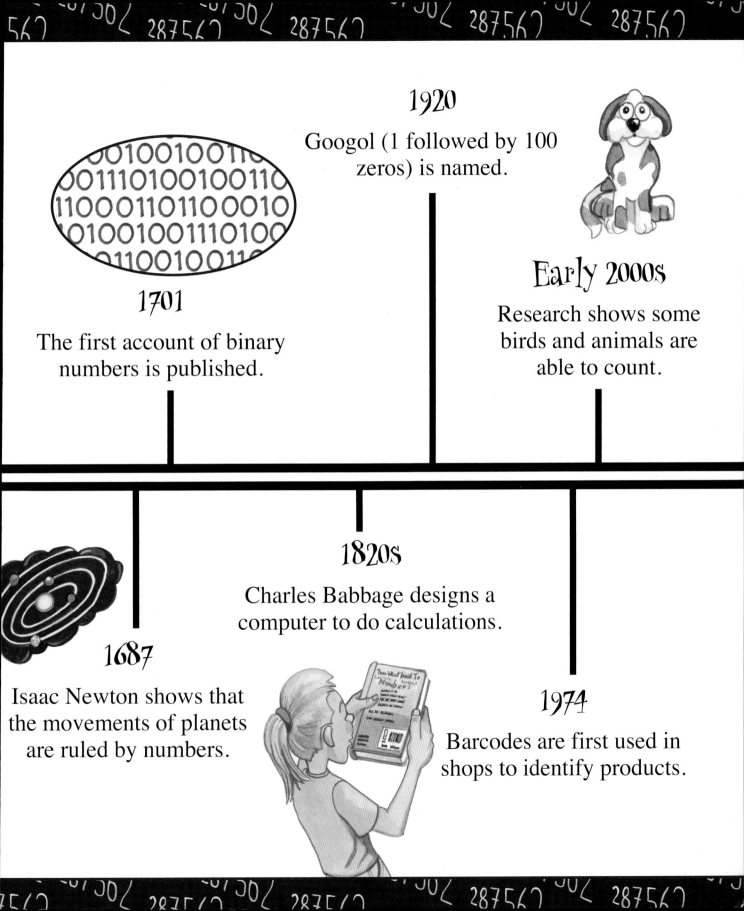

**1920**

Googol (1 followed by 100 zeros) is named.

**1701**

The first account of binary numbers is published.

**Early 2000s**

Research shows some birds and animals are able to count.

**1820s**

Charles Babbage designs a computer to do calculations.

**1687**

Isaac Newton shows that the movements of planets are ruled by numbers.

**1974**

Barcodes are first used in shops to identify products.

# Number systems around the world

Our own number system using 0 to 9 developed in India and the Middle East over the last 2,000 years. But there have been many others.

In ancient Babylon, people used a system based around 60 – this is why we have 60 minutes in an hour. In ancient Rome, the system was based on 10, but written with letters: I (1), V (5), X (10), L (50), C (100), D (500), and M (1,000).

The Oksapmin people in New Guinea base their counting system on 27 body parts. The Mountain Arapesh language of Papua, New Guinea, counts coconuts, fish and days using a system based on 3, but nuts, bananas and shields using a system based on 4. The ancient Mayan civilisation in Central America used a counting system that was based on 20.

*(Ancient Rome)*
*Roman numerals*

*(Ancient Babylon, Iraq)*
*Base-60 counting system*

*(Iraq)*
*Arabic numerals*

*(Oksapmin people, New Guinea)*
*Body-counting system based on 27 body parts*

*(Ancient Mayan civilisation, South Mexico/Central America)*
*Base-20 counting system*

*(India)*
*Zero first used*

*Author:*

**Anne Rooney** studied English at Cambridge University, England, and then earned a Ph.D. at Cambridge. She has held teaching posts at several UK universities and is currently a Royal Literary Fund fellow at Newnham College, Cambridge. She has written more than 150 books for children and adults, including several on the history of science and maths. She also writes children's fiction.

*Artist:*

**Mark Bergin** was born in Hastings, England, in 1961. He studied at Eastbourne College of Art and specialises in historical reconstructions, aviation and maritime subjects. He lives in Bexhill-on-Sea with his wife and children.

*Series creator:*

**David Salariya** was born in Dundee, Scotland. He has illustrated a wide range of books and has created and designed many new series for publishers in the UK and overseas. David established The Salariya Book Company in 1989. He lives in Brighton with his wife, illustrator Shirley Willis, and their son Jonathan.

*Editor:* **Jacqueline Ford**

*Editorial Assistant:* **Mark Williams**

PAPER FROM
SUSTAINABLE
**FORESTS**

Published in Great Britain in MMXVII by
Book House, an imprint of
**The Salariya Book Company Ltd**
25 Marlborough Place, Brighton BN1 1UB
www.salariya.com
www.book-house.co.uk
ISBN: 978-1-911242-29-1

1 3 5 7 9 8 6 4 2

A CIP catalogue record for this book is available from the British Library.

Printed and bound in China.

Visit our website at **www.salariya.com** for **free** electronic versions of:
**You Wouldn't Want to be an Egyptian Mummy!**
**You Wouldn't Want to be a Roman Gladiator!**
**You Wouldn't Want to be a Polar Explorer!**
**You Wouldn't Want to sail on a 19th-Century Whaling Ship!**

# You Wouldn't Want to Live Without™

# Numbers!

Written by
## Anne Rooney

Illustrated by
## Mark Bergin

Series created by
## David Salariya

## BOOK HOUSE
*a* SALARIYA *imprint*

# Contents

# Introduction

How much do you like numbers? Maybe you enjoy number games? You might not like numbers as much when you have to do your maths homework, but it would be really hard to live without them. You wouldn't just miss out on puzzles and games.

Imagine how difficult life would be if you couldn't count things, measure anything, do any calculations, or be precise about time, distance or price. You wouldn't know how old you are, or how long you have to wait until your holiday. We couldn't build anything accurately, we'd have no computers, no accurate recipes, no scores in games or sports. You really wouldn't want to live without numbers!

*Biscuits*

*Ingredients:*
*Some flour*
*Some sugar*
*Some eggs*
*Some butter*

*Instructions:*
*Mix and bake in*
*oven until done!*

# What are numbers?

Numbers give us a way of showing quantity – how many or how much, how long, and so on. Examples of numbers are 'two', 'thirty-five' and 'six-hundred thousand'. We write numbers down using the digits 0 to 9. A numeral is a set of digits used to write a number. So 2, 35, and 600,000 are all numerals. We use numbers for lots of different purposes. We use them to count, to carry out calculations, to measure things, and as labels. Numbers are also used in codes.

ARE NUMBERS REAL?
Philosophers argue about whether numbers and the rules of maths are real or just a human invention. Does it matter? What do you think?

A CASTAWAY on a desert island might use numbers to count how long they've been marooned!

NUMBERS ARE GOOD for counting objects – but they don't give you any other information, such as size or quality. Is one big thing the same as one small thing? It is if you're just counting!

MEASURING. Some things – like time, distance and speed – can't be counted, so we have to measure them instead.

# You can do it!

Try to spot all the places you come across numbers in a day – from your alarm clock to the cereal packet and bus timetable.

PHONE NUMBERS and car registration plates use numbers to identify things – every phone or car has a different number.

CODES AND LABELS. In a shop, the barcode on anything you buy is a number. The number is a special code that tells the shop what the item is.

WE CALCULATE with numbers in lots of areas of work, such as engineering, building, science and art. These calculations are often used to keep us safe.

TRADE – buying and selling things – uses numbers all the time. Prices and interest rates, special deals and discounts are all parts of the way we buy and sell things, and they all rely on numbers.

# Does it add up?

**B**efore people used named numbers, they used tallies. A tally matches things one-to-one, with one thing representing another. Imagine you were a shepherd. You might use one pebble to represent one sheep. You'd need the same number of pebbles as sheep. If you drop a pebble into a pot for each sheep that passes, it's easy to see if you've got all the sheep. If there are pebbles left over, some sheep are missing. Tallies are a good way of keeping track of things.

IF THE TALLY doesn't match the number of the objects, and you can't count, then you won't know how many sheep are missing or how many to look for.

YOU CAN OFTEN see if one group is larger than another without having to count. Even some animals can do this, too. Lions will only attack a smaller pride, and they will run away from a larger pride.

FINGER-COUNTING is a bit like tallying, but you don't need any extra objects. Each finger is equivalent to an item; you could hold up five fingers to show you have five chickens.

Another sheep, another pebble...

If you're making a tally, it's easiest to draw vertical lines for the first four, then draw a bar across those lines for '5', then start again with more vertical lines.

NAME THAT NUMBER. Giving names to the numbers means you can count without using stones, sticks, fingers or any other aid.

SOME BIRDS, as well as hyenas, chimpanzees, fish and frogs, have a basic understanding of numbers. Birds can tell if any of their chicks are missing, for example.

HEAD TO TOE. If you used toes as well as fingers you could count to twenty. But the Oksapmin people of New Guinea do even better. Their body-counting system assigns numbers to 27 different parts of the body!

13

# Where did numbers come from?

oday, we use a 'place value' system for writing numbers. This means the position of each digit tells us how much it is 'worth'. The digit on the right shows the units (ones), the next digit to the left shows the number of tens, the next digit to the left shows how many hundreds, and so on. So when we write '653', it really means (6x100)+(5x10)+(3x1). It's a very simple way of writing large numbers. But it's not the only method that has been used. Some older number systems were much harder to work with.

THE PLACE-VALUE system means we can write really big numbers by just adding more and more digits.

THE NUMERALS 0 to 9 that we use today came originally from India, and were then used by Arab mathematicians in the Middle East and North Africa.

THE ROMANS USED LETTERS to build up numbers: I (for 1), V (5), X (10), L (50), C (100) and M (1,000). They repeated I, X, C, and M as necessary, so II = 2, III = 3, VII = 7 (5+2), XXXI = 31 and so on. To keep the numbers a bit shorter, they had another trick; IV = (5–1) =4, and IX = (10–1) =9. It could get rather complicated!

**You can do it!**

Try to write out the date of your birthday using Roman numerals in the form dd-mm-yyyy (day-month-year).

III IV MMVI

LONG MULTIPLICATION. Imagine trying to do sums with Roman numerals – there's no easy way!

**Why is this so hard?**

PEOPLE IN EUROPE used Roman numerals until after 1200, when the mathematician Leonardo Fibonacci brought Arabic numerals to Italy. Arabic numerals didn't really become popular until the 1400s, even though they made maths much easier.

**No! One, not ten!**

EARLY NUMBER SYSTEMS didn't use 'zero' at the end of numbers. That made it hard to tell the difference between 4 and 40, or 6 and 600. Imagine how confusing that would be!

NUMBERS NEVER END – they are infinite. We can carry on writing larger and larger numbers, even writing numbers so large that they don't refer to anything in the universe.

# How many is 10?

We count using a base-10 number system. That means that we first count from 0 to 9, and then we start a new column for 10s (with a 1) and reuse the same digits to count higher (10, 11, 12...) When we get to 19, we increase the number in the 10s column (which becomes 2) and start again with 0 in the units column (20). We probably use base-10 because we have ten fingers. But it's not the only way to count. Any number can be used as a base.

A HUMAN ASTRONAUT and an alien that used base-7 would not agree about how to write a number of objects. The astronaut would say there are 16 eggs, but in base-7 the alien would write this as 22 (2x7+2). There would still be just as many eggs, however it was written!

ANCIENT BABYLONIANS based their number system on 60. You can still see signs of this today: we divide a circle into 360 degrees (6x60) and an hour into 60 minutes.

THE MAYANS used a system based on symbols for 1 and 5, and worked in base-20.

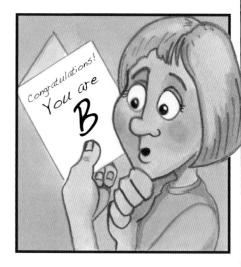

COMPUTERS OFTEN USE base-16, because this means they can store large numbers in less space. Letters are used as digits for the numbers 10 (A) to 15 (F).

AN ALIEN WITH seven tentacles might count in base-7 (see below). They would count 0 to 6, then start again, with 1 in the 7s column and 0 in the units column. So 10 would be 7, 11 would be 7+1=8, 12 would be 7+2=9, and so on. After 13, the alien would increase the 7s column to 2 and count 20!

## How it works

Not all measurements are based on counting in tens – many older measurements are not. For example, a foot has 12 inches, and a pound has 16 ounces.

1,2,3,4,5,6,10!

# What if you can't count?

Imagine you wanted to buy some rice. You wouldn't ask for 4,000 grains and wait for them to be counted, would you? It's much easier to measure the rice in some way, such as weighing it or measuring its volume. Or what if you wanted to buy orange juice for a picnic? You really can't count orange juice. When things can't be counted, we measure them instead. We measure anything that is continuous, like distance or liquids, and things that come as very small particles, like rice, sand or flour. Many grocery items are also measured by weight, such as nuts and sweets.

How can it be the same amount?!

SAME MEASURES. It is important that we all agree on the measures we use. A big bucket does not hold the same amount as a small bucket. If we all used different measures, we would argue all the time.

86, 87, 88...

18

That's 113 feet.

No, it's 97 feet!

## How it works

There are lots of different units of measurement. Some are rather odd. The heat of chilis is measured in Scoville heat units (named after American pharmacist Wilbur Scoville, who created this form of measurement).

WHOSE FOOT? Measures need to be consistent so that we can compare them with each other. If a foot is used as a measure of distance, we need to choose whose foot – otherwise we won't be able to agree on the distances we measure.

SOME MEASURES HAVE large and small versions. We measure the length of a bug in millimetres, but the distance to the sun in millions of kilometres.

JOURNEY TIMES. How we measure things can change. Distances used to be measured in the time it took to travel, not the distance covered – it was a more useful thing to know.

Two days.

How far to Rome?

ONE SIZE FITS ALL. A person can't be in more than one place at a time. So to use someone's foot to measure things, we make a standard – a copy that stands in for the real foot, and is used by everybody.

19

# Putting numbers to work

**W**ith numbers, we can do all kinds of calculations. Whenever we make anything, we measure and calculate distances, angles, areas and volumes to make sure that things fit together properly and are strong, stable and safe. Architects and engineers measure forces and stresses. It takes a lot of numbers to get complex systems like rockets, planes and cars right. A tiny wrong calculation can mean the system doesn't work – and that could lead to disaster. Numbers are really important!

WE HAVE LIFTOFF! A space rocket launch involves a lot more numbers than just a countdown. Maths is central to getting it right.

We have a total payload of 28,800 kilograms.

It will reach a maximum thrust of 4,500 kilonewtons.

T + 20 seconds
Speed: 28,000 kph
Altitude: 200 m above sea level

Numbers let you compare things. Measure your hand span, and that of nine friends or classmates. What is the range (smallest to largest)?

ONCE PEOPLE STARTED to own and fence in land, they needed to measure it. In ancient Egypt, the river Nile flooded every year. The Egyptians had to measure out their fields all over again after each flood.

THE I-35 BRIDGE over the Mississippi River collapsed in 2007 because it wasn't strong enough – the engineers had got the maths wrong.

FORECASTING THE FUTURE. We count and measure things over time to make predictions. Knowing there are more storms helps us to measure climate change and plan for the future.

NUMBERS GIVE US the power to change things. By counting and comparing over time, we can work out which animals are in danger and work to save them.

IF WE MEASURE lots of examples of something, we can work out what is normal and what to expect in the future. We can work out averages – and spot things that are unusual.

SAVE THE TIGER

Height

Weight

# Less than zero

ounting and measuring works when you have things to count or measure, but what happens when you don't? Negative numbers help you to count things you don't have! If that sounds strange, think about what happens if you borrow something. Imagine you borrow an orange from a friend and eat it. You promise to give your friend an orange the next day. You now have less than no oranges, because as soon as you get one you have to give it away. You have minus one (-1) orange!

Brrrr! -30°C today!

SUBZERO. When numbers are used for a scale, they often go below zero. A thermometer shows negative numbers for very cold temperatures.

IF PEOPLE BORROW money to buy something, they have the thing, but they now have a negative amount of money, as they have to pay back what they borrowed.

**Top tip**

How cold does it get in winter where you live? Is it a negative number? Draw a chart to show what you will need to wear at different temperatures.

IF YOU KNOW you should have eight sheep but can only find five, add more sheep below zero on the number line until there are eight in total. You can see there are three still to find.

IN SOME COUNTRIES, the ground floor in a building is numbered zero because you don't have to go up or down to be on it. Below the ground floor, the floors have negative numbers because they are below zero.

GAME OVER. In some games, you can lose points by making a mistake. It's even possible to get a negative score if you're not very good at it, because you can lose more points than you win.

IS ZERO A NUMBER? If you have none of something, is that really a number? There are so many things you have none of – no pet elephants, no spaceships, no toy clowns...

# Numbers, codes and labels

**N**umbers can be used for more than counting, measuring and calculating – although all those things are pretty useful. They can serve as labels or codes, too. When they are used in this way, they have nothing to do with maths. Numbers are great for codes because you can keep adding more and more. Numbers used as codes and labels are all around us, from the channel numbers on the TV to the number on the door of your house or flat.

COMPUTER CODE. Computers turn everything into a code made of numbers. So whether you're using the computer to write stories, look at videos or edit your photos, it's all turned into numbers inside.

PHONE NUMBERS are not entirely random numbers. They include codes that show the region where the phone is registered or the network it uses.

*Top tip*

To decide whether a number is used as a code, work out whether you would do maths with it. You wouldn't add up house numbers, would you?

IN A CATALOGUE, every item has a code that identifies it. There might be barcodes to scan, too. A database stores all the information about an item under its number.

TV CHANNELS are identified by a number – but it's just a code. There is no real reason why a channel should have one number rather than another.

IDENTIFICATION. Lots of things are identified by numbers, from books to cars. Each item is given a special number – its own unique code. There's even a unique code on every book that identifies it to booksellers and libraries.

COLOUR CODED. Sometimes numbers look like a code but are actually a kind of counting. RGB numbers tell a computer the amount of red, green and blue needed to make up a particular colour on the screen.

25

# Do you have the time?

What time do you get up? What time does school end? How long are your classes? When's the next bus? How old are you? We measure and talk about time constantly, and we use numbers for it. It's not just for hours of the day, but also for the date in the month, and the year. If we didn't have numbers it would be really difficult to keep track of time, or plan when to do things. Without numbers, it would be much harder to talk about what we've done during our day, or what we did in the past or hope to do in the future.

PRECISE TIMES MATTER. From catching the school bus to finishing your test in the time you're allowed, clocks help us keep track of when to do things, and when to stop doing things.

A YEAR IS the length of time it takes the Earth to go around the Sun, and a day is the time it takes the Earth to rotate. So there really are 365 days in a year – that's not a human invention!

# You can do it!

At the weekend (not on a school day!) try living without looking at a clock or your watch all day. Eat when you're hungry and sleep when you're tired. Does it seem strange?

**Happy New Year!**

BUT NOT QUITE. There are actually 365.25 days in a year. It would be really inconvenient to start a new year part way through a day, so we have leap years to use up all the extra quarter days.

NUMBERS AND TIME. Since we show times using numbers, we can also calculate with them. We can work out durations (how long something takes) and intervals by adding and subtracting times.

## SCHOOL TIMETABLE

|  | START | FINISH |
|---|---|---|
| MATHS | 9:00 | 9:45 |
| Length of class: 45 mins | | |
| HISTORY | 10:00 | 10:45 |
| Length of class: 45 mins | | |
| SCIENCE | 11:00 | 12:00 |
| Length of class: 1 hour | | |

| STATION | SCHOOL | PARK |
|---|---|---|
| 9:00 | 9:20 | 9:45 |
| 10:30 | 10:50 | 11:15 |
| 12:00 | 12:20 | 12:45 |
| 13:30 | 13:50 | 14:15 |

TIMETABLES USE NUMBERS to show the time when things start and finish, or when trains or buses get to different places. Without a timetable, you couldn't plan your journey.

HOW OLD? We count our age in years and use numbers to record dates. How would you know how old you were without numbers?

# Precisely

Numbers give us a way of being precise. They help us to work out chances, probabilities and proportions, making life less risky and unpredictable. They let us set limits and guidelines to keep ourselves and each other safe.

Lots of aspects of safety depend on using precise numbers: not too much and not too little of something. We make choices all the time depending on levels of risk and probabilities.

DOCTORS CALCULATE the doses of medicine needed for big people and small people. Too little won't make you better, but too much could be harmful. With the help of numbers, they can get it just right.

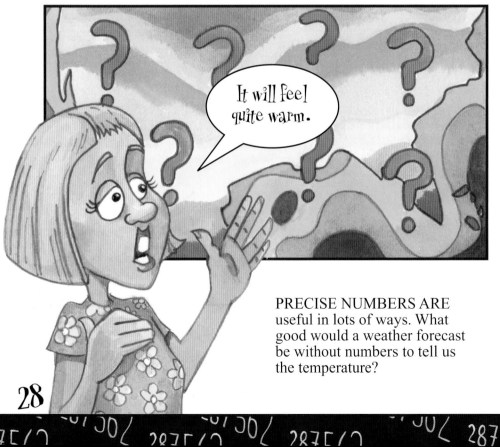

It will feel quite warm.

PRECISE NUMBERS ARE useful in lots of ways. What good would a weather forecast be without numbers to tell us the temperature?

NOT TOO FAST

SAFETY IN NUMBERS. Numbers let us set limits and guidelines to keep people safe. What if we had no speed limits, or no safety limits for electrical items? We could act dangerously without knowing it.

WHAT ARE THE CHANCES? Probability is a measure of how likely something is to happen. If you had to pick one marble from a bag containing one black marble and four white ones, the chances of getting a black one would be one in five, or $\frac{1}{5}$.

**Top tip**

Probability is just a guide: it doesn't tell us exactly what will happen. If there is a 90% chance of rain, it still might not rain.

IS IT WORTH IT? Probability helps us compare risks and benefits. You're more likely to enter a difficult race for a 10 percent chance of winning a bike than a 10 percent chance of winning a chocolate bar.

YOU CAN WORK OUT numbers from proportions. If you know half the children in a class of 30 like sandwiches, you need $\frac{1}{2}$ x 30 = 15 sandwiches. Without numbers, you'd end up with too many or too few – and a fight!

A PROPORTION IS part of a whole group – it's a fraction. If an animal shelter had 90 dogs and 30 were brown, the proportion of brown dogs would be 30÷90, which is the same as $\frac{1}{3}$ (a third).

# Numbers don't need us

**W**hether or not we use numbers ourselves, the universe follows mathematical rules. Nature uses patterns, ratios, symmetry and shapes that we describe using numbers and mathematics.

The rules of nature have always been there and will continue to be there forever, even if we stop using numbers or cease to exist.

## The Fibonacci Sequence

**NUMBERS IN NATURE.** Numbers make patterns everywhere in nature. One you can easily spot is the 'golden spiral'. It crops up in shells, plants and fruit. Nautilus shells often show the spiral clearly. If you trace the nobbles on a pineapple or the seeds in a sunflower head you'll see they are packed into the same widening spiral pattern.

**THE FIBONACCI SEQUENCE** is a special series of of numbers that lies behind many patterns in nature, including the golden spiral. It was discovered by Fibonacci (see page 15). The number of petals flowers have is usually a Fibonacci number.

1, 2, 3, 5, 8, 13, 21, 34

$$0+1=1$$
$$1+1=2$$
$$2+1=3$$
$$3+2=5$$

$$5+3=8$$
$$8+5=13$$
$$13+8=21$$
$$21+13=34$$

**THE FIBONACCI SEQUENCE** is the series of numbers: 1, 2, 3, 5, 8, 13, 21, 34... and so on. The next number is found by adding up the two numbers before it.

BEES PACK HONEY into hexagonal (six-sided) cells. It's one of the best shapes for filling an area without gaps. Also, hexagons are extremely strong and don't bend out of shape under pressure.

## You can do it!

Make your own symmetrical snowflake from paper. Fold a circle of paper in half and then into thirds, and cut a pattern into the sides. Open it out to see your snowflake.

THE MOVEMENT OF the planets is controlled by the gravity of the sun and the other planets. They were all in the right places long before Isaac Newton worked out the laws of their movement in 1687.

NATURE LIKES SYMMETRY. Most animals have two-fold symmetry like us. If you could fold yourself in half along the length of your spine, your right and left halves would match.

SPEEDING IN SPACE. The universe has a speed limit – nothing can go faster than the speed of light: 299,792,458 metres per second. A spaceship going that fast would take 4.2 years to get to the next nearest star.

SNOWFLAKES ARE SYMMETRICAL in a special way. They are made of a section repeated six times, rotating around the centre.

31

# So, would you want to live without numbers?

**N**umbers are everywhere in our lives, even places we can't see them or don't notice them. We are so used to them we rarely even think about how important they are. Numbers and calculations are essential to making and running the things we use every day. Without numbers used in mathematics, we couldn't make safe buildings or machines. We couldn't schedule our time, use money, have computers or understand science. You really wouldn't want to live without numbers!

LET'S TRADE. Without numbers for prices, we would have to barter – swapping things we already have for things we want. It's not very efficient – what if no one wants what you have to offer?

IF WE COULDN'T measure time, it would be difficult to arrange anything. But people did manage to arrange to meet up before the invention of clocks!

IMAGINE ALL THE things we wouldn't have if we didn't have numbers. Numbers are vital in designing, making, testing and running lots of things we take for granted.

Try going for a day – or even a few hours – without using numbers. Which things can't you do? How hard is it?

NUMBERS HELP TO keep us safe. Without them, we wouldn't be able to make anything accurately – things such as cars and buses might not work properly, and buildings might fall down.

Three!

IF WE EVER encounter aliens, they might have a completely different number system and way of doing maths. Perhaps it's possible to express the same rules in different ways – but they would still be the same rules, however they are described.

33

# Glossary

**Architect**  Someone who designs structures such as buildings and bridges.

**Babylonian**  A person who lived in the ancient city of Babylon, now in Iraq. The Babylonian civilisation was destroyed about 3,500 years ago.

**Database**  A collection of data (raw information) stored together on a computer in a way that means it can easily be searched or sorted into a different order.

**Digit**  A single number character, 0 to 9.

**Discount**  The amount by which a price is reduced in a special offer.

**Engineer**  A person who designs machinery, structures or equipment using a variety of materials.

**Interest rate**  The rate at which extra money is charged when someone borrows a sum of money. The person pays back the original sum borrowed, plus an extra amount – perhaps 5 percent or 10 percent a year of the total they owe. The extra is called 'interest' and is a charge for borrowing.

**Interval**  The time that passes between two events.

**Leap year**  A year in which February has 29 days; in non-leap years it has just 28 days.

**Mayan**  Relating to the culture of the Maya in Central America. The Mayan number system was first used 3,000 years ago. The Mayan civilisation was destroyed 500 years ago.

**Negative number**  A number that is less than zero; it is shown by putting a minus sign (-) before the number.

**Number line**  A line showing numbers, equally spaced, going up from zero towards the right (positive numbers) and down from zero towards the left (negative numbers). It can be used to help with calculations such as addition and subtraction.

**Numeral** A number written down using digits; 43, 891 and 5,139 are all examples of numerals.

**Place-value system** A system of writing numbers which involves assigning value to a digit according to its place (position) in the number. In our place-value system, the final digit (on the right) represents units (ones), the next to the left represents tens, the next hundreds, and so on.

**Prediction** What someone expects to happen, usually based on caclulations or another form of evidence.

**Probability** The likelihood that something will (or will not) happen, expressed as a decimal fraction between 0 and 1, or as a percentage.

**Proportion** A portion or fraction of a group, expressed as a fraction (a half, a quarter) or a percentage.

**Symmetry** The state of a shape being the same when folded, reflected or rotated in one or more direction.

**Tally** A way of keeping score or count by using objects or making marks to correspond to the item or event being tracked – such as making a mark on the wall of a cave to record each day of being marooned on an island.

# Index

# Amazing number facts

## Infinite infinities

There is no end to numbers – they go on forever. Infinity is the word we use to describe the numbers that go beyond what we are able to count. But there is more than one infinity. You could also count forever (to infinity) going *below* zero, which would be a negative infinity. And there are infinite decimal fractions between every pair of numbers. It's enough to make your brain spin!

## Googol and googolplex

The names for really large numbers, like billion and trillion, follow a rule that uses set prefixes (bits at the start of the word). But there are some special large numbers with their own names. A 'googol' is 1 followed by 100 zeros (written $10^{100}$). And a googolplex is 1 followed by a googol zeros (written $10^{googol}$). The name 'googol' was invented by nine-year-old Milton Sirotta in 1920. He was the nephew of mathematician Edward Kasner.

## Sagan's number

The number of stars in the observable universe is known as 'Sagan's number', named after the astronomer Carl Sagan. The trouble is, we don't really know how many stars there are. When the number was first named it was thought to be around 10 sextillion ($10^{22}$). By 2010 it had risen to 300 sextillion – that's a lot more!

## Amazing Sums

Some sums are fascinating:

$$111111111 \times 111111111 = 12345678987654321$$

and

$$12+3-4+5+67+8+9=100$$

# Top counting aids

If you just count and calculate on your fingers, you can't get very far. Even adding toes doesn't help much. So people have used lots of different aids to help with counting.

**Abacus**  An abacus is usually a wooden frame of rods threaded with beads. One row represents ones, the next tens, the next hundreds and so on. Numbers are counted or calculated by moving beads in the different rows. Abacuses of various designs have been used for around 4,000 years.

**Counting board**  It's possible to make something like a simple abacus using just pebbles and dips in the sand or a board of wood. This is called a counting board. We don't know when they were first used, as dips in the sand don't last long!

**Quipu**  A quipu is a counting aid made of knotted strings. A thick string has thin strings looped over it, and then coloured strings knotted around the hanging strings, so it looks rather like a tangled, sparse fringe. It was used in South America by the Inca people but we don't know exactly how they used it, as they had no written language.

**Calculator**  The French mathematician Blaise Pascal made the first mechanical calculator in 1642, but the first one to be manufactured and sold appeared in 1851. The first electronic calculator was introduced in the 1960s. It's already impossible to imagine life without an electronic gadget to help us do sums, whether it's a computer, calculator or smart phone.

# Did you know?

Standardizing measures is difficult unless you already have a standard! Long ago, people used hollowed-out gourds (a kind of vegetable like a squash or melon) to measure volume. To compare different gourds, they filled them with seeds and then counted how many seeds each could hold.

If you wanted to count to a million, saying one number each second and counting twelve hours a day, it would take just over 23 days. But if you wanted to count to a billion, it would take more than 63 years!

The decimal point that we use to show the decimal part of a number is fairly new. Previously, the decimal was shown by a bar drawn above that part of the number. And in France, a comma is used instead of a decimal point (e.g. 34,5).

Some measures that have the same names in the USA and the UK are actually different amounts. In the USA, a pint is 473 millilitres (ml) while in the UK it is 568 ml. To make it even more complicated, in the USA it matters whether you measure something wet, like water, or something dry, like sand. A 'dry pint' is 551 ml.

When we talk about big numbers we use lots of vague words such as 'umpteen', 'shedloads' and 'gazillions'. Sometimes, we even use precise numbers imprecisely – 'dozens of' doesn't usually mean sets of 12, even though a dozen is another way of saying 12.